The
SPUR BOOK
of
CAMPING

The
SPUR BOOK
of
CAMPING

by
Terry Brown and Rob Hunter

A
SPURBOOK VENTURE GUIDE
SPURBOOKS LIMITED

Published 1976 by
SPURBOOKS LIMITED

6 Parade Court
Bourne End
Bucks

ISBN 0 904978 06 0

Printed by Maund & Irvine, Ltd., Tring, Herts.

PUBLISHER'S INTRODUCTION

"Any Fool can be uncomfortable"

This is a book about basic, simple, camping. It is based on the "me and my pal" principle, which the authors learned years ago in the Commandos, but it is also written in the belief that a knowledge of basic camping skills is essential for all those whose hobbies and pursuits take them out of doors in all weathers. This book will enable outdoor enthusiasts to equip themselves for camping, and get them started on living out of doors.

In common with the other books in this series, "KNOTS"; "MAP AND COMPASS"; "SURVIVAL"; "FIRST AID"; "SNORKELLING"; and so on, it is based on the idea that the subject covered is a means to an end, as well as an end in itself.

There exists a vast range of literature on Camping for Campers, the people who like to spend their holidays under canvas. Given wheels, car, truck or trailer, the holiday camper can develop his hobby until he is virtually going away with a canvas house, complete down to the television.

Our book is aimed at those who, while they enjoy camping, camp as part of some other outdoor activity, as Scout, Rambler, Climber, Potholer, Back-packer, Fisherman or Naturalist. These people camp because it is cheaper, because there are no hotels where they wish to go, because they have a large hotel-repellent dog, or because it is simply more fun.

Just how much fun, or otherwise, camping is in practice, depends on the camper having a good basic knowledge of camping and outdoor living techniques. Such techniques are the subject of this book.

As there is, quite literally, no limit to the amount of kit that *can* be bought and transported by car or trailer, and the refinements are endless, we have gone back to basics without too much stress on very lightweight camping, or back-packing. You can develop the kit and information in this book to your heart's content. Here you will find the basic information, with a few useful tips besides, essential reading for the outdoor man.

LIST OF CONTENTS

Publisher's Introduction

Chapter 1

WHERE TO CAMP

In the United Kingdom anyway, all land, even common land, belongs to, or is controlled by, someone. To camp there without permission, means being a trespasser, and eventually being ordered off. You ought to camp in a designated camping area, or get permission first.

DESIGNATED CAMP SITES

There are a number of books and paperbacks, published annually, which list official or organised camp sites. The most popular of these are *Cades Camping Site Guide*, and the Link House, *Camping Sites in Britain*. Most camping magazines like *Practical Camper* and *Camping* give lists and up-to-date information on camp sites. The magazines also give the novice camper a good deal of up-to-date hints on techniques and equipment.

Official bodies like the Forestry Commission, the National Trust, and the National Parks Commission, all have camp sites in their preserves and will provide you with the information upon receipt of a request and a small fee. They also charge for the use of the camp site.

Organisations such as the Scouts, Guides, Youth Hostels Association, and above all, the Camping Club of Great Britain at 11, Lower Grosvenor Place, London SW1, are also sources of information and have their own organised camp sites. The same holds good, to a greater or lesser degree, for most organisations where their activities necessarily take their members anywhere remote

Designated camp sites have one great advantage—usually—over just kipping down where you stop, and it may be summed up in one word—lavatories. If you camp anywhere other than on an organised site, and frequently there too, you'll have to take particular notice of the toilet facilities—or lack of them.

FREE CAMPING

By this we mean pitching camp anywhere other than on a designated site. Here again, you ought to ask permission, and if you don't know who to ask let us suggest the following:

Consult the O.S. map for the region in question, and find a suitable site. The names of farms are usually shown and you can make a fair guess as to whose land the site is on. The maps usually show the name of the farm, and you can write a polite letter to the farmer, assuring him of your experience and tidiness, and ask permission to camp on his land. Enclose a stamped addressed envelope for his reply. This usually works, and even a 'NO' saves you wasting time. Another idea is to ring the local Police and ask their advice. They know everyone and are usually helpful, and can put you onto someone who has no objection to campers.

Finally, if all else fails, you can go and camp and chance your arm. Provided you do no damage, you will, at worst, be ordered off. In a densely inhabited rural area, free camping is difficult, but if you are up a mountain, deep in a wood, or out on a moor, it's unlikely that you'll be bothered. A parting thought though, is that you should respect other people's property, be friendly, and observe the Country Code, doing no damage, and leaving no litter.

CAMPING IN EUROPE

As a general rule the camping facilities in Europe, especially France and Germany, are much higher than those in the U.K. The weather helps, of course, and camping is an excellent way of seeing Europe at moderate cost. In Germany the Black Forest and Bavaria are excellent regions; in Italy, the Lakes and the Italian Riviera.

In France, Brittany and Normandy are full of excellent camp sites of all sorts, while for really warm weather, you need to head south of the Loire, to the Auvergne, Burgundy, the Dordogne Valley, or the wild plateaux and mountains of the remote region of Languedoc-Roussillon, south of Toulouse. Camp sites in France are plentiful, well appointed and cheap. The Michelin Camping Guide gives full details, as will the French Government Tourist Board, 178 Piccadily, London W1.

Chapter 2

TRAINING AND EQUIPMENT

Camping isn't really taught; it is something you learn. There are organisations, like the Scouts, and Outward Bound Schools, which teach camping techniques to their members, and in the case of Outward Bound, run courses for outsiders. It is best to learn a little about camping first, before you invest in equipment, so that you have a fair idea of the type of camping you enjoy, which, in turn, dictates the type of equipment you should buy.

Most people learn the basics by going off with an amiable friend who shows them the ropes (literally), and then learning more from other campers. Also, fortunately, camping is one of those skills you can actually learn from a book. Unlike most activities, camping is non-competitive, which makes campers a friendly crowd, and advice and assistance is aways forthcoming. One useful tip, used on the Continent even by experienced campers, is that you should, if possible, camp next to Germans, and then look helpless. Unable to endure this painful spectacle for long, they will bustle over and with gutteral cries, have your tent up, lilo inflated and sleeping bag organised in a trice, while their wives give you the first of many cups of excellent coffee. We thought this tip was a joke, but it actually works!

The secret of successful camping, as with most skills, is organisation and practice. You will quickly learn the right and wrong ways to go about things, and if in doubt or trouble, our advice would be, ask another camper. If none is about, then use your commonsense.

EQUIPMENT

HIRING

Initially, camping isn't cheap. An adequate set of equipment for two people can cost about £150. Buying good equipment that will last, ensures that this cost can be amortised over several years, but the initial expenditure can hardly be avoided.

However, an excellent alternative exists, for you can hire camping equipment, and in the early days, when you are not sure if you will like camping, and lack the experience to know what equipment is best suited to your particular purpose, then hiring is a very good idea.

Most camping goods shops operate a hire service and you can obtain a list of hirers from the Camping Club, or from the classified advertisements in the camping journals. If, after hiring equipment, you decide to purchase it, the hire fee is usually remitted, and hirers often have a stock of used equipment that can be purchased at a considerable discount. End of season sales are worth attending.

BUYING SECOND-HAND

There is a strong streak of Mr. Toad in many people. Great enthusiasts, they decide to take up a sport, buy all the latest gear, and then they lose interest in it and another set of expensive equipment moulders in the garage. This is particularly true with camping. If the wife or children have a nasty encounter in the night with a creepy-crawly, the family camping ends abruptly. Incidentally, if you *borrow* equipment, be sure it is suitable. We once borrowed a tent to go summer camping in the New Forest, only to find out when we got there that to erect it you needed two pairs of skis!

Local newspapers, newsagents' notice boards, or such publications as *Exchange and Mart*, often contain advertisements from people wishing to dispose of second-hand, barely used, camping gear, and this does give the novice camper a chance to pick up a few bargains. In addition, you can take the initiative and advertise for equipment yourself, specifying your requirements precisely.

HOW TO BUY

When negotiating with the seller, find out exactly what he has for sale. Insist on seeing the tent erected, when you can check for tears, missing guys or pegs and, of course, see and learn how to erect it yourself. Examine zips. Check cooking equipment for rust, and stoves for leaks, a pressure stove with no pressure is useless. If you know the brand name and type of gear on offer, which you should find out before the actual inspection, you can, by checking with existing catalogues, make a reasonable guess at a fair asking price for second-hand gear. Provided you inspect the items carefully, and are certain they are what you need, then purchasing second-hand equipment can be a considerable saving.

EQUIPMENT PURCHASE: SOME CONSIDERATIONS

Camping is full of knick-knacks, and there is no end to the range and variety of gear.

If you have a car or a trailer you can take what is, in effect, a canvas house, complete with bath and television. Since you *can* do this, elaborating the equipment, with only transportation as the limiting factor, we, in this book, are going to cover the basics. Not what you can have, but what you can't do without.

We are basing our requirements on those for two people, man and wife, sister and brother, boy and girl, me and my pal. Camping is more fun with a companion, and if you are going anywhere remote, you should certainly not go alone.

WEIGHT

The great limiting factor is **Weight.** The total weight that the **average** fit person will want to carry all day without exhausting himself is somewhere within 20 and 30 lbs (9–14 kilos), and preferably the lower figure. Therefore, bearing in mind that the outdoor man may need to carry gear for his own particular pastime as well, binoculars, cameras etc., plus food, we are suggesting here, camping equipment weighing no more than 25 lbs (11 kilos). Two people can therefore carry 50 lbs (22 kilos) which should be more than adequate (Figure 1).

FIGURE 1

WHAT DO YOU NEED?

Item	Weight
Tent x 1 (include flysheet)	8 lbs
Sleeping bags x 2 (Icelandic)	6 lbs 4 ozs
Lilo/mat x 2	6 lbs 12 ozs
Rucksack/backpack x 2	5 lbs
Stoves x 2 (Optimus or Gaz)	3 lbs 8 ozs
Water bottles (plastic, empty)	— 5 ozs
Cooking gear x 1 (aluminium)	1 lb 4 ozs
Eating gear x 2 (plastic where possible)	1 lb
Torch x 2	1 lb 8 ozs
Spare clothes/track suits—socks, sweater, underwear x 2	8 lbs
Spare shoes, plimsolls x 2	3 lbs
Washing/shaving etc. x 1	1 lb
Survival: space blanket/first aid kit x 1	1 lb
Survival food x 2	2 lbs
For two people =	48 lbs 9 ozs

Now these weights are approximate, taken from up-to-date (1976) catalogues, for good, but not excessively costly gear. You can perhaps omit some items, and you may care to add others. We have checked this list with campers and camping stockists and it does cover all the main requirements for two people camping.

All the above gear would go in the rucksack, backpack or sac. In addition we would expect the camper to wear walking shoes or boots, anorak and cap and walking trousers, and carry in his pockets, map, compass, and have round his neck a camera or binoculars—all additional weight.

The above does not include food and water, which you may be able to obtain locally, though you will almost certainly need to carry some. Try not to carry lots of tins but use dehydrated foods. There is the advice, well-known but worth repeating, of the camper who, after a trip divided his gear into three piles; the gear he had used a lot, the gear he had used a little, and the gear he hadn't used at all. On his next trip he left the third lot at home, but took all the first plus a careful selection from the second. It helps to remember that whatever you take, weighs.

You can get the weight down by paying more. You can get tents, the major heavy item, weighing no more than 4 lbs., but they are expensive. You may need only one stove or one torch. Try and make every weight saving you reasonably can. We believe that a balance must be struck between weight and an adequate range of items. All the above items you will need. You can economise and save weight and may choose to do so, but if you work around the figures above, you won't go far wrong. Now let's look at these items individually. The range of brands is vast, so take particular note of those requirements which affect the equipment, whoever the manufacturer.

Chapter 3

TENTS

Tents come in various types, ridge, frame, mountain, arctic or lightweight, and an ever widening range of shapes (Figs. 2 & 3). Get advice on the right type for you, before you consider size. Here we illustrate a two-man, ridge tent which is still the most popular type of tent for most purposes. The basic requirements for a two-man ridge tent is that it should have walls, a sewn-in groundsheet, and a flysheet, the latter incorporating a porch. Tent fashions change continually, so consult a competent stockist, and choose the best you can afford.

Suitable tents with these features exist in the **Blacks 'Good Companion'** range, the **Y.H.A. 'Venture'** series, the **Vango 'Force Ten'**, and many more. Most of these tents are either all nylon, or have a cotton, inner tent, and a nylon or polyurethene-treated flysheet. With nylon, you increase the risk of condensation, especially in cold weather, or at altitude, but it is light and rain resistant.

Study the diagram (Fig. 4, Page 16) for the names of the parts.

BUYING A TENT

The tent inner: Buy a good make. Try and see it erected. Camping exhibitions, large stockists, or camp sites provide opportunities for this. Get inside and stretch out. Is it suitable for the camping you have in mind? Ask advice on this, for it can be vital, especially if you intend to camp high in the hills. Study the seams of the tent. Are they well stitched, and the corners and guying points secure? Has the tent adequate ventilation? Does the inner door zip up easily? Has it a fitted, tough groundsheet? Does it, in short, look well made, sturdy and workmanlike? Is it high enough? The tent should have walls at least 12" high and more if possible, and two of you should be able to sit up in it comfortably. Walls greatly increase the amount of room in a tent, and you can stow gear along the walls leaving the centre clear for sleeping and living in. For camping in moderate conditions, we recommend the ridge tent of the type shown in the drawing (Fig. 4), but tents nowadays come in a variety of shapes. If you buy a ridge tent, a ridge-pole stops the tent sagging in the middle.

The flysheet: A flysheet covers the main tent, acting as a shield against wind and rain, and helps to keep the tent cool in summer, and warmer in winter. Although you *can* get tents, especially lightweight ones, without flysheets, don't. Always have a flysheet. They add considerably to both weight and cost but we consider they are worth it. You will find it most useful.

The flysheet should be rainproofed, and have a 'porch' or extension to give protection at the entrance. In the shelter thus provided, you can, on rainy days, put the flysheet up first, erecting the tent underneath in the dry, and later do your cooking. Gear can be left here, and bulky equipment stowed around the flysheet, outside the main tent (Fig. 2).

FIGURE 2

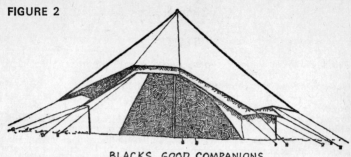

BLACKS GOOD COMPANIONS

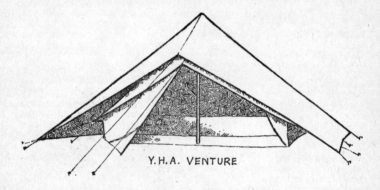

Y.H.A. VENTURE

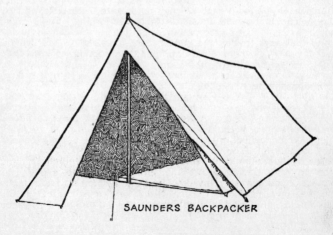

SAUNDERS BACKPACKER

FIGURE 3

VANGO FORCE 10

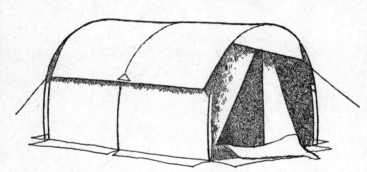

BLACKS NYLON TUNNEL TENT

BLACKS MOUNTAIN TENT

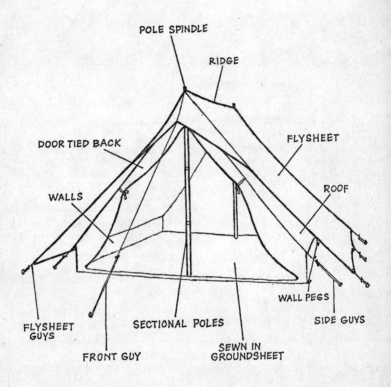

POLE SPINDLE

RIDGE

DOOR TIED BACK

FLYSHEET

WALLS

ROOF

FLYSHEET GUYS

WALL PEGS

SECTIONAL POLES

SIDE GUYS

FRONT GUY

SEWN IN GROUNDSHEET

FIGURE 4

16

The flysheet, when fitted, should not touch the inner tent at all, and needs to have separate guys. Be sure to peg down as low as possible, for if the wind springs up in the night, the flysheet will flap away, all night, and drive you mad!

Quite apart from its role as part of the tent, the flysheet can serve as a temporary shelter during a lunch halt, or be used to cover you in a sudden rain storm. In emergencies you can use it to wrap up your pal if he gets a touch of exposure.

Groundsheets: As we have just seen, you can use a flysheet for roles which, a few years ago, were filled by the groundsheet. This is because nowadays, most tents have fitted groundsheets, sewn round the bottom of the main canvas, and a very good thing too.

Fitted groundsheets make the tent easier to erect, for you just peg out the groundsheet and put in the poles. They help keep the tent warm, as they keep out draughts around the tent bottom, and they help to repel creepy-crawlies, which makes them especially popular with the ladies.

Fitted or not, your groundsheet should be of a tough rubberised canvas or PVC, stout enough to repel the rising damp, and tough enough not to tear if you scramble over it in nailed boots. Lightweight campers will obviously go for lightweight tents. The range is vast, so consult a good stockist.

When you strike the tent, be sure to clean the damp grass or mud off the underside of the groundsheet. If possible throw the tent over your rucksacks for a few minutes, and let the sun dry off the underside before you pack it away. When you first buy your tent, erect it in the garden and leave it up for a few days to weather.

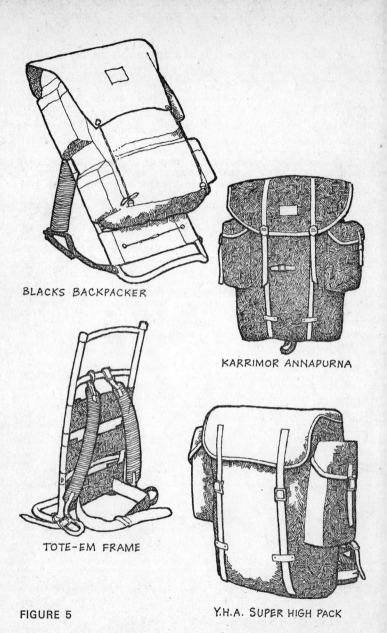

BLACKS BACKPACKER

KARRIMOR ANNAPURNA

TOTE-EM FRAME

Y.H.A. SUPER HIGH PACK

FIGURE 5

18

Chapter 4

RUCKSACKS, BACKPACKS, FRAMES

While you are buying your basic camping equipment, you will also need something to carry it in. For most people this means a rucksack, a backpack, or a pack frame, in nylon or canvas, and as there is a wide choice, we should discuss these now, before we buy the rest of our camping gear (Fig. 5).

A poorly made, unsuitable or badly fitted rucksack can, when filled and heavy, be absolute torment to the person humping it. So try it first, and load in some gear to see if it is still comfortable when full.

FIT YOUR FRAME

Most rucksacks and backpacks are carried on frames. You should have a frame, and be sure it fits you comfortably, with the sack itself held just clear of your back, which allows air to circulate and prevents sharp objects inside digging into you.

The frame should rest comfortably on the hips, and the top of the frame should be level with the top vertebrae (Fig. 6). This, if the sack is properly packed, which we will cover later, should ensure that the weight is kept high, borne on the shoulders, and not dragging you back. A final tip is that the frame should detach from the sack. Frames are an awkward shape, and if you travel by car, or hitch-hike, or go canoe-camping or sailing, you will find it easier if you can separate the frame and sack for stowing.

THE SACK

Sacks get a lot of rough treatment and you must check that the one you buy is of strong material, that the seams are well stitched, and that the sack has good big pockets. Straps and buckles are better than zips. Check that they are strongly stitched to the fabric. For weight saving, nylon has obvious advantages, although canvas is still popular, and very strong. The sack should preferably be waterproof and the outer pockets should have gussets. Flat pockets are of little use.

The shoulder straps will carry a lot of weight, and should be well padded. If the straps are unpadded, you can make pads out of foam rubber, to protect the shoulders. If the frame fits, you can buy sacks in different sizes, for different loads, thus allowing you to vary the length of your trip away from civilisation. Be sure the sack is big enough to hold all the kit. Don't have mugs or packets dangling outside. Keep your gear in the sack, and it will be dry and secure.

WHICH TO CHOOSE

Rucksacks and backpacks are available in a wide variety of shapes and sizes, suitable for a variety of purposes, and you need to consult a competent stockist and inspect a wide selection before choosing. Don't pick the first one you see. The Commando Bergan rucksack is sometimes available from Army surplus stores. This is a tough, canvas rucksack, but a trifle heavy.

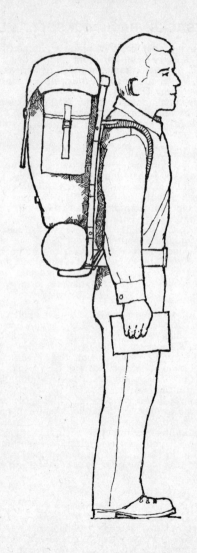

FIGURE 6

The Blacks Backpacker is a large rucksack, moderately priced at around £12, and weighs only 1.36 kg (3 lbs).

The Karrimor range which includes rucksacks, pack frames and climbing sacs, has been used on many expeditions and is popular with mountaineers, while the Y.H.A. have an attractive range of rucksacks suitable for the camper and rambler, and all moderately priced.

You must make up your own mind but remember that the rucksack must be framed, well-stitched, have straps, not zips, with gussetted pockets, and preferably be light. As with tents, to get lightness with strength, costs money, but as a rucksack will last you for years, it will be money well spent.

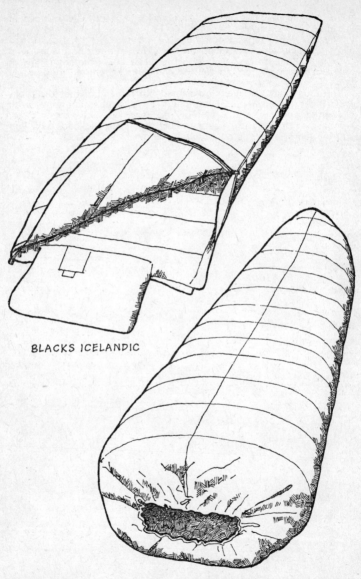

BLACKS ICELANDIC

POINTFIVE SNOWCAP

FIGURE 7

22

Chapter 5

SLEEPING BAGS

Once again, you have to think ahead and consider what sort of camping you intend to do.

Sleeping bags are expensive, and you will not want to buy a range of bags to cater for a variety of climatic conditions.

Assuming you will not be out in the severest winter conditions, but anticipating all the same that unexpected hard weather can strike, you can still draw on a wide range of bags which should meet your requirements.

CHOOSING YOUR BAG

You need a sleeping bag to keep you warm while sleeping! Simple! The critical element in achieving this aim is the filling, and this falls into two main areas; natural and synthetic. Natural fillings, down and feathers, are the best, but expensive. A synthetic filling with man-made fibres like Dacron, is usually adequate. Avoid Kapok, which can become lumpy. The next element to consider is the stitching of the bag, which greatly affects the insulation.

The bag needs to be stitched into compartments, to keep the filling deployed all over the bag. The best form of stitching, found on the best bags, is overlapping stitches. Then comes 'walled' stitching, and last but still adequate, quilting. Examine the stitching on the bag before purchase. (See Fig. 8.)

Some bags have zips, others only a draw string at the neck. Zips are fine unless they jam or break. Personally, we recommend a zipped bag, with a full length zip, then if you have a summer-weight bag and get caught in severe conditions you can zip two bags into one. Apart from certain obvious advantages, two people in one bag is a lot warmer than two separately. If you are cold, in a snow-hole for instance, it's quite surprising how many people can cram into a bag. Full length zips do provide a large cold spot.

One point about bags is to get one big enough. If you get into a small bag and zip it up, it's rather like being in a coffin, and the feeling is very claustrophobic.

Get a bag wide enough for your shoulders, and be sure you can turn in it without rolling over, bag and all. Use a sleeping bag liner. Buy two, and keep them clean. They keep the bag clean, and since it will then not need cleaning so often, this increases the life of the bag. Most bags need to be dry cleaned. Check this before you have it washed and, after dry cleaning, air the bag thoroughly. Cleaning fluid fumes can be dangerous.

WHICH TO CHOOSE

Consult your stockist, tell him what you intend to do, and ask his advice. A good quality bag for normal summer camping, will cost between £15 and £25. You can pay much more for arctic or sub-zero bags. Popular brands are the Blacks Good Companion, or Icelandic bags, which weigh between 3 lbs and 4 lbs (1.5 to 2 kg).

The buyer needs to check the filling, the quilting, the size, and the weight.

Remember that, apart from camping, a sleeping bag can often be used to bed down an unexpected house guest. The same emergency use holds good for a lot of camping equipment.

SLEEPING PADS, MATS, AIR-BEDS

Years ago, in the Commandos, we could sleep on rocks, or in mud, quite easily. Those were the days! Sleeping in beds is bad training for a night on the cold hard ground, so for a good night's sleep, you need to put some sort of cushion between you and the deck. There is nothing 'cissy' in this. Remember, any fool can be uncomfortable.

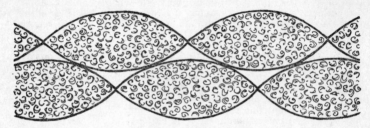

2 LAYERS OF SIMPLE QUILTING

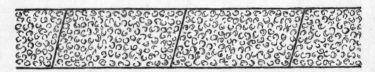

BOX WALL

SIMPLE QUILTING

FIGURE 8

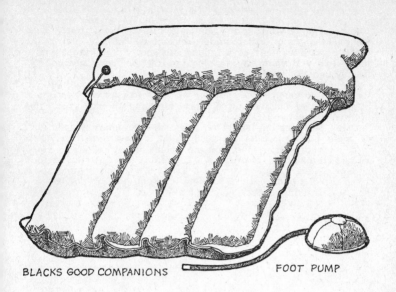

BLACKS GOOD COMPANIONS   FOOT PUMP

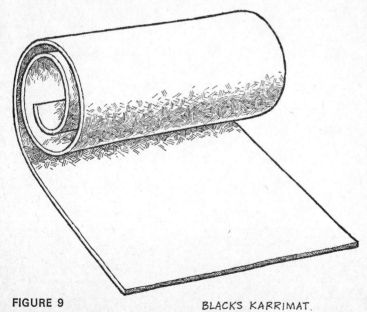

FIGURE 9   BLACKS KARRIMAT.

25

Pads or mats are light and adequate, but somewhat bulky. They are made of foam, and provide excellent insulation, which is the other great advantage of a ground cushion. Apart from comfort, they keep you warm, by keeping you off the damp ground. We usually use an airbed.

The airbed needs to be long enough to support the bulk of the body, although for weight and packing reasons you can obtain a short airbed that will just support hips and shoulders, and this is often quite adequate.

Camp beds, or the low safari beds are sometimes popular with campers but the struts are easily bent, awkward to carry, sink into snow or soft ground, and are somewhat strenuous to erect. They also take up a lot of room in the tent. We recommend a good pad or airbed, weighing around 3 lbs (1.5 kg) and costing about £7. If it has a pump, use it. Blowing up a bag on lung power alone can be shattering, especially at high altitudes.

Chapter 6

STOVES

Once you have ensured a good night's sleep, you can turn your thoughts to breakfast and a stove to cook it on. Camping stoves fall into three main types; gas, petrol/paraffin, and solid fuel. Each has its devotees, but the most popular nowadays are either the gas cookers of the blue camping gaz types, or pressure cookers from Primus or Optimus (Fig. 10).

FUELS

Gas is clean, self-contained, very reliable, and handy to pack (Fig. 10). On the other hand you will need to carry spare containers, which adds to the weight and the refills are not cheap. Pressurised gas containers are not permitted on aircraft. The gas normally used is butane. Butane will not burn below freezing point, and in the mountains, in the early morning, the temperature, even in summer, can be below this. If you intend to camp in all weathers at altitude, you should consider a petrol or paraffin pressure cooker of the Primus/Optimus type (Fig. 10). These are sturdy, reliable, and cook quickly and well. If the stove has a wind-shield, so much the better. The snags are that you need also to carry fuel, which can spill and contaminate your food and clothes, there is an increased fire risk, and you will need to service the cooker regularly, and carry spare parts, especially 'prickers' to keep the fuel vent clear.

Some campers prefer solid fuel stoves, as they are light and compact. They are, however, slow cookers, and you should not use solid fuel inside a tent. It gives off terrible fumes. If you cook at all inside the tent you must beware of fire, and take special precautions against flames and flying fat. Before purchase, get the stoves demonstrated. Nothing is more miserable than lugging a stove up a mountain and then not being able to use it.

If you use a paraffin stove you will need to prime it with methylated spirits to get it going. Petrol stoves need no priming, but then petrol is a more volatile, dangerous fuel. Never fill a stove inside the tent, or anywhere at all while smoking.

The Optimus 'Mouse Trap' gas stove is very light, and ideal for the mid-day brew.

You have, therefore, when purchasing a stove to consider the type of camping you have in mind, and the relative snags and benefits of the different type of cooker. On balance, for everyday use, we would come down on the side of gas. It is cleaner, easier to pack, and generally more convenient.

FIGURE 10

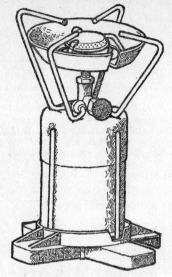

BLUET S.200 STOVE

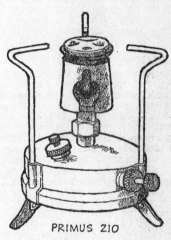

PRIMUS 210

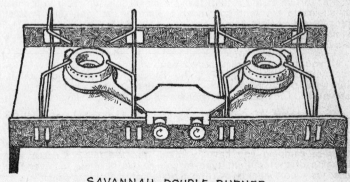

SAVANNAH DOUBLE BURNER

A FEW TIPS

Two burners are three times more useful than one. So either have a double burner stove or, better still, two single stoves. Then you have a spare if one goes wrong. We have allowed for this in our 'me and my pal' list of stores. Note the amount of time you have had the burner on, and mark the time in indelible pencil on the side of the container. The small Camping Gaz container, for example, lasts for about three hours, and you need to know how much cooking time you have left.

Wind will greatly reduce the amount of heat actually cooking the food, so shield the flame from the breeze. This is where a porch, on the tent flysheet, comes in handy. Otherwise you will need to erect a small windbreak, of stones or kit. Above all, don't forget the matches, and/or, a lighter.

Once again, if the weather is really foul, and you cook inside the tent, be careful of fire, and leaking fuel. Finally, again, never refill a petrol or paraffin container inside the tent, when smoking, or near a naked flame.

CAMP FIRES

We don't recommend camp fires. Frequently they are not allowed. Unless you are careful there is a risk of sparks igniting dry grass and the fire spreading. Collecting wood can take ages, and of course if it is wet then life becomes that bit harder.

Probably the worst part of cooking by wood fires is that the pots get into a frightful mess.

However, if you *must* have one, make sure that it is permissable and use only dead wood or, if you are by water, drift wood. Collect a good supply and remove the turf, if any, from where you intend to lay the fire. See Fig. 11 for details.

Make sure the fire is out before you leave and replace the turf.

CHOPPING WOOD

It is not recommended that you go around chopping down trees. If you *are* in the unlikely position or being allowed to and wish to then do it as Fig. 14. When chopping wood use a block or tree stump and chop out v-shaped segments as in Fig. 14. Keep the axe covered or sink it into the block.

FIGURE 11

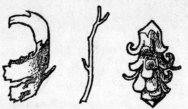

LIGHT FIRE USING PAPER, CARDBOARD, FIR CONES, CURLS OF BIRCH BARK, DRY TWIGS OR STICKS SHAVED AS SHOWN AT RIGHT.

GET FIRE GOING AS A TEEPEE SHAPE WITHIN BRICKS, STONES OR 2 GREEN LOGS.

KEEP A SUPPLY OF FUEL HANDY.

WAIT UNTIL THERE ARE GLOWING EMBERS TO COOK BY.

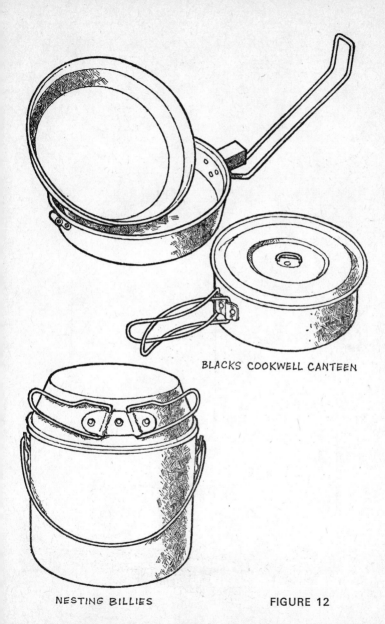

BLACKS COOKWELL CANTEEN

NESTING BILLIES

FIGURE 12

31

FIGURE 13

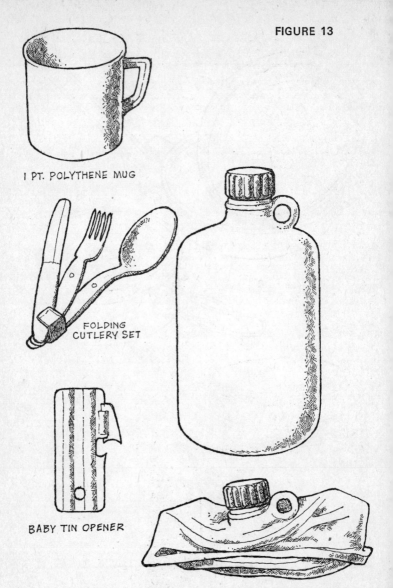

1 PT. POLYTHENE MUG

FOLDING CUTLERY SET

BABY TIN OPENER

COLLAPSIBLE 1 GAL. BOTTLE

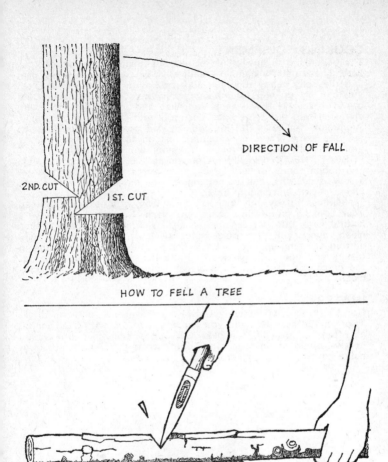

DIRECTION OF FALL

2ND. CUT

1 ST. CUT

HOW TO FELL A TREE

WHEN CHOPPING STICKS
HOLD ON A BLOCK AND
CHOP AWAY FROM
YOUR BODY.

MAKE SURE THERE
IS NO ONE BEHIND YOU

FIGURE 14

COOKING EQUIPMENT

The best thing to buy is one of the aluminium, non-stick, canteen sets. These usually contain a saucepan, or two, and a frying pan, and they clip neatly together, and pack away tidily. With this set you can fry up eggs and bacon, stew meat or warm soup, and brew up tea. This will keep you alive and fed, and the talented chef can turn out some excellent grub with just these few items. Aluminium foil is useful for cooking and covering unused items, so take some. There is of course no end to the bits and pieces you can get, but one piece of equipment is essential. DON'T FORGET THE TIN OPENER. A plastic spatula for turning the eggs and bacon comes in very handy, and weighs nothing. Don't forget a few dishcloths, and something to dry the dishes. If you can, take a plastic washing-up bowl.

Needless to say, but we'll say it anyway, it is essential to keep your cooking and eating equipment clean. Non-stick gear is very helpful here, but you can use earth or sand to scour your dishes clean, even with only cold water available. This will save you carting washing-up liquid about. For carrying water, for washing dishes and yourself, a fold-up canvas bucket is very useful. Get the grease off first with sand or earth before you swill the dishes clean.

WATER

Don't assume that water will always be available, or fit to drink. Take limited supplies with you and top them up with fresh water, as often as possible. The best and lightest container is a plastic screw-topped bottle containing about two quarts. You need about half a gallon per person per day as a minimum.

Chapter 7

OTHER ITEMS

INSURANCE

As we mentioned, camping equipment is not cheap. Have it insured for loss and damage up to the full value of the kit, and revise the premium annually. You should also consult your insurance people to be sure that you are covered if you indulge in outdoor pursuits. Europe Insurance of Croydon, Surrey, specialise in insuring camping kit.

SOME USEFUL SUNDRIES:

First Aid Kit: This should contain plasters, anti-hystamine ointment (for stings), bandages, lint and aspirin. Know First Aid. (See the Spur Book of Outdoor First Aid 1976.)

Sealing Tape: Take some adhesive tape. If you tear the tent you can make a quick repair.

Torch: We have one each, of the hand type, that can be hung up for reading or placed on the ground, when working in the dark.

Cleaning and Packing: Take some plastic bags and J-cloths; you'll find them useful.

Plastic Bags: Take some for bringing your rubbish home. Don't leave plastic bags where animals can eat them, for (heaven knows why) cows like plastic!

Matches: Don't forget the MATCHES.

Safety Pins: Handy for sealing tents, bags or trousers if zips fail.

DON'T FORGET the tin opener; bottle opener; corkscrew; toilet paper.

Maps and Compass: Have the appropriate maps, O.S. 1:50,000 and a Silva Compass. Know how to use them. If you don't, can we recommend the SPUR BOOK OF MAP AND COMPASS (75p) which gives all the necessary information.

Knife or Axe. For longer established camping, chopping firewood and so on, an axe is handy. However, weight being a problem, we recommend a good, heavy knife, with a broad-backed blade like the American Bowie knife. This is heavy enough for hammering in pegs, and can be used for chopping wood. Whether knife or axe, keep it sharp. Sharp tools are safer than blunt ones.

Trowel: For burying spoil. You don't really need a mallet as pegs can usually be heeled in, or use rocks.

CLOTHING

Camping, in itself, needs no special clothing. The way you dress will depend on whatever activity your camping is designed to support. The normal outdoor rig consists of anorak, smock or cagoule with lots of pockets, a woollen jumper, woollen shirts and trousers, well-washed socks which are less likely to blister your feet than new, unwashed, ones, and suitable footwear for moor or mountain. Be sure your boots are comfortable, and well broken in. The same basic clothing is suggested for both sexes.

FIGURE 15

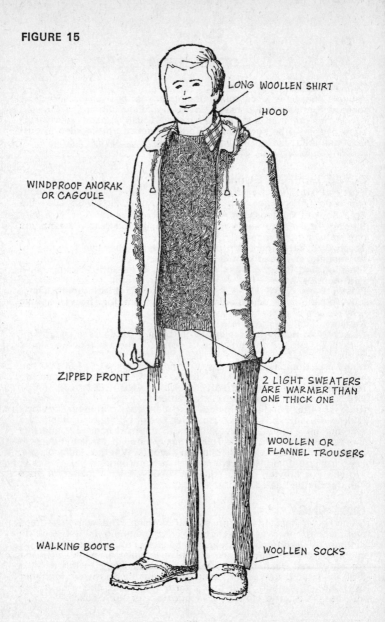

LONG WOOLLEN SHIRT

HOOD

WINDPROOF ANORAK OR CAGOULE

ZIPPED FRONT

2 LIGHT SWEATERS ARE WARMER THAN ONE THICK ONE

WOOLLEN OR FLANNEL TROUSERS

WALKING BOOTS

WOOLLEN SOCKS

You will, however, need one complete change of clothing, in case you get wet. At the end of the day, and for first thing in the morning, a track suit is very suitable, and worn with a pair of gym-shoes, is just right for lounging around the tent. Some people take pyjamas!

IF YOU GET WET

If you get wet early in the day, stay wet. Keep your dry clothes for the night. You might decide to change wet socks for dry ones, as wet socks can soften and then blister your feet; but for the rest, stay wet. Walking in wet clothes will not hurt you, you will stay warm, and they will eventually dry on you. Sleeping in wet clothes will, at best, give you rheumatism in later life. If, however, you change your wet clothes for dry ones, at once, you may finish the day with a rucksack full of wet heavy clothes. So, stay wet, put on dry clothes in the tent and at night, and if you have to, put on the wet ones again in the morning. Few things sort out the men from the boys more quickly, than putting on wet clothes in a snow hole!

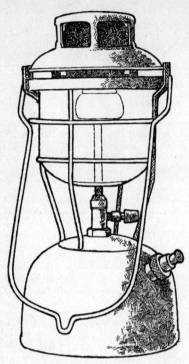

TILLEY STORMLIGHT

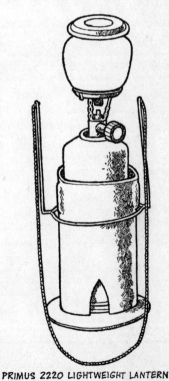

FIGURE 16

PRIMUS 2220 LIGHTWEIGHT LANTERN

Chapter 8

LIGHTING AND HEATING

We haven't included lights in our basic list, because they are really a frill. If you go to bed at dusk and get up at dawn, you won't need much artificial light, and a good chat is a lot more sociable than reading. You can read a little with a torch if you really must.

There is, however, a case for carrying some illumination, and if you want to bear the extra weight, it's up to you (Fig. 16).

The first tip is to use the same fuel for lighting as for cooking. It saves duplication and extra weight. Remember to have good ventilation inside the tent, if you have a lamp or stove lit inside.

CANDLES

Don't use candles. In a tent they are dangerous, and unless shielded they blow out easily, and drip wax. The only exception would be in a snow hole. A small candle in a snow-hole, with the beam reflected from the snow crystals, gives a brilliant light. But, with this exception, no candles.

HURRICANE LAMPS

These burn paraffin, are more secure, and give an adequate light, and some heat. Be sure the wick is clean, and the glass polished. Pack it carefully, and fill and light it **outside** the tent.

TILLEY LAMPS

a tilley lamp will give an excellent light, especially when the pressure is pumped up. It's not particuarly light in weight, and you need spare mantles, but if you really need a good light to work to after dark, it cannot be bettered. It will burn all night on one filling of paraffin.

CAMPING GAS LAMPS

These burn off gas cartridges and give a good light. The Lumogaz comes in a range of sizes and one will suit you.

HEATING

The best form of heating is good equipment, warm clothes and a hot meal. Otherwise you can buy a small heater, running off one of the fuels listed above for lighting. Heating a tent shouldn't be necessary and is rarely successful. It increases condensation, and unless you are off to the Arctic for which you need very special equipment anyway, leave heating stoves at home.

Chapter 9

PERSONAL HYGIENE AND LATRINES

Keep yourself clean. It not only makes you a more agreeable companion, it is healthier, and more comfortable. People who wander around unshaven and scruffy, may imagine they look tough and rugged; actually they just look dirty.

WASHING

You will need to take with you one set of soap, shaving gear, toothbrush (2) and paste. These should be in a sponge bag or, better still, a plasticised hold-all with pockets and tapes long enough to go round the waist. You then tie it round you to wash in river, trough, or bucket, and don't have to put your soap down in the mud.

These can sometimes be found in Army Surplus Stores, and they last for years. Otherwise you can make one. (See Fig. 17.)

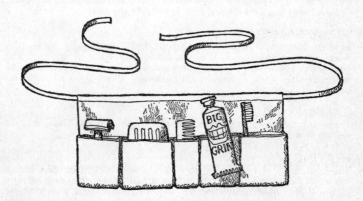

FIGURE 17

LATRINES

Wild animals, which live their entire lives out of doors, never foul their own ground. Neither should we. The lightweight camper, if on the move, can water the flowers as he goes and no great harm is done, and he can perhaps take advantage of cafe or pub lavatories at least once a day. If no pub presents itself, you should retire to cover, dig a hole and fill it in afterwards.

In a more permanent camp site, greater care should be taken with the siting of latrines. Urinating all over the place should be discouraged. The latrine should be sited downwind, in a sheltered spot, away from washing and drinking water, and dug out to about two feet deep. Leave the earth piled up neatly where everyone can, with a spade, cover up his spoil, and keep the flies off. Flies spend their lives flying between open latrines and food. Even in the country, wash your hands frequently.

Chapter 10

GOING CAMPING

The secret of successful camping, apart from practice, lies in planning and organisation. Make out lots of check lists, listing all the items you **Need**, rather than those you would merely like. Lists prevent you leaving things at home—well, sometimes!

CHECK LISTS
For a trip which involves camping, you will **need** (for two people) the following items:

> Rucksacks (2)
> Tent and flysheet (1)
> Sleeping Bags (2)
> Liners (2)
> Air beds (2)
> Stoves (2)
> Fuel
> Torches (2)
> Batteries
> Cooking gear (1 set)
> Eating gear 2 sets)
> Spare clothing
> Tin opener (2)
> Bottle opener 1)
> Corkscrew ((1)
> Matches (2)
> Maps, Compass (1)
> Safety Gear (as applicable)
> First Aid Kit (1)
> Washing and cleaning gear
> Food

The type and weight of the individual items depends on your pocket and preferences. Remember to save weight, even in small ways. For example take two toothbrushes, but only one tube of toothpaste.

FOOD
Deciding what food to take is a permanent problem. Whatever you take will have to be carried, so first of all consider if food and water supplies are available within reach of your camp site, or if you can eat your main meal of the day in a pub or cafe. There is no need to be Spartan if you don't have to. You may not need to cook either, for on short trips you can take pre-cooked food that only needs heating up.

However, in remote districts you will need to carry food and probably water. The problem then is to decide what and how much, and the best way to do this is to prepare a meal chart.

	DAY 1	DAY 2	DAY 3	SUNDRIES	TOTAL SHOPPING LIST
Breakfast	4 eggs 4 sausages 2 slices bread 2 mugs tea	4 eggs 4 rashers bacon	4 eggs 4 rashers bacon	Butter (lb) Salt Tea bags (6) 1 large loaf	1 doz eggs 1 lb butter ½ lb sausages 1 large loaf Salt 8 rashers bacon (l lb)
Lunch	2 teas 2 apples 2 cheese sandwiches	2 teas 2 oranges Ham sandwiches	2 apples Corned beef sandwiches Tea	1 lb apples 2 lb oranges Tea bags (6)	1 lb apples 4 oranges 1 lb ham ½ lb corned beef
Dinner	Meat stew 2 teas	Steak and Kidney Pie Rice pudding Tea	Spaghetti Bolognese 2 oranges Tea	Tin opener Sugar Tea bags (6) 2 oranges	1 tin stew 1 tin steak and kidney 1 tin spaghetti bolognese 1 tin rice pudding
Supper	Biscuits 2 teas	Ham sandwiches Tea	Biscuits Tea	Biscuits Tea bags (6)	1 packet biscuits 24 tea bags Sugar Water (?)

The meal chart takes about 10 minutes to prepare, provides the basis for a shopping list and gives a fair idea of the weight involved.

In the case of the meal chart shown here it amounts to three days' rations, less water, and weighs about 10 lbs (4½ kilos) which is not too much if divided among two people. Try and save weight by taking packaged soups and stews rather than tinned foods whenever possible. Try to have a reasonably mixed diet, with some fruit and roughage.

In these days you won't get scurvy, but you can get constipated!

EMERGENCY FOOD

If you are going into remote country, or mountains, especially in uncertain weather, you must, in addition to those foods you expect to consume, take emergency rations.

Chocolate, some packet soups, porridge, sugar and tea, cheese, barley sugar, dried fruit, all have a high calorific content, weigh little and will keep. Put the emergency rations in the bottom of the rucksack, and keep them for emergencies. Incidentally, if you are going into rough country you should have at least three in the party.

PACKING THE RUCKSACK

You must pack it so that the weight is evenly distributed, and you can get items out as you need them, without having to unpack the whole lot. It follows that you must remember where things are, and it is best therefore to have a standard method of packing your rucksack and stick to it (Fig. 18).

Maps, compass, etc., can be stowed in the pockets of the rucksack, but are best kept in your anorak pocket. You don't want to be forever opening and closing the rucksack pockets.

There are five general rules. First, pack in the reverse order to your unpacking requirements. That is, the things you will, or may, need first, you put in last. Second, get the heavy items as high in the sack as you can. Third, put breakables where they are protected. Fourth, stop metal objects rattling, it will drive you mad. Fifth, make a list and tick off items as you stow them away.

So, put the tent in last, put your lunchtime food in an outside pocket, and put stove and fuel handy for a mid-day brew. Once you strap up the sack in the morning, it should stay shut till the evening. Once you have packed the sack, put it on and hump it around for a while. Then make any adjustments necessary to get it comfortable.

TIME, DISTANCE, WEATHER

You must consider *where* you are going to camp, and factors such as the weather, the terrain, and the time of year.

Study weather reports and forecasts, and take appropriate gear and precautions. If you are going to a remote area let someone know your route and destination. Do not try and do too much, especially when unfit, inexperienced, or with young children.

Aim to stop at least two hours before dusk.

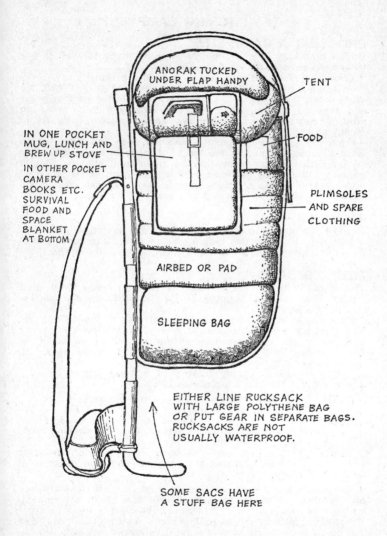

ANORAK TUCKED
UNDER FLAP HANDY

TENT

IN ONE POCKET
MUG, LUNCH AND
BREW UP STOVE

FOOD

IN OTHER POCKET
CAMERA
BOOKS ETC.
SURVIVAL
FOOD AND
SPACE
BLANKET
AT BOTTOM

PLIMSOLES
AND SPARE
CLOTHING

AIRBED OR PAD

SLEEPING BAG

EITHER LINE RUCKSACK
WITH LARGE POLYTHENE BAG
OR PUT GEAR IN SEPARATE BAGS.
RUCKSACKS ARE NOT
USUALLY WATERPROOF.

SOME SACS HAVE
A STUFF BAG HERE

FIGURE 18

45

Chapter 11

PITCHING CAMP

CHOOSING A CAMP SITE

On an organised site, the choice may be made for you If you have a choice, consider the following points:

Choose a sheltered site, not in a hollow or long grass, away from hedges and not under trees. Hollows hold ground mist, are often damp, and can flood. Long grass and hedges harbour gnats and assorted insects, while trees will drip heavily on you long after rain has stopped, and have been known to fall in gales. Avoid muddy ground.

Pitch the tent on flat ground with the open end facing down wind. Choose dry soil, in the lee of a copse or stone wall. And so on! There are so many tips on choosing a site that if you tried to find a place that met even half of them, you'd be up all night! Remember the enemies are wind and rain. Take precautions against the effects of both and you won't go far wrong (Fig. 19).

FACILITIES

Has the site access to water, fresh food and lavatories?

You need to know this **before** you go there. Once on the site, consider where you will cook, and wash, and site the latrines.

PITCHING CAMP

The object is to get the tent up, all the gear ready for a good night's sleep and a meal going. To do this effectively and quickly, you need a **Routine.**

How you erect the tent depends on what sort of tent you have. You should know how to erect it swiftly, even in the dark. If it's very windy, one of you can lie on the tent, giving advice, while the other pegs in the groundsheet and hammers in the pegs. But, as with everything, have a routine (Fig. 20).

Your routine will clearly depend to a great degree on your equipment, but for us it is usually as follows:

BOTH: Take off rucksacks and place in sheltered spot. Erect tent; put rucksacks inside.

ROB: Takes off boots, enters tent. Hands out stores and cooking gear. Inflates airbeds, unpacks sleeping bags, arranges tent, finds torches, lights lamp.

TERRY: Prepares cooking site, lights stove, puts on water for a brew, prepares tins and cooking gear. Gets meal ready.

Given that a routine exists, you can get it to the point where all the above takes no time at all. We can be inside the tent, eating stew, in less than 15 minutes. The time it takes to erect the tent depends on the tent. They come in all shapes these days but be sure you know how to erect it before you set out.

If it is raining, or windy, then it is even more important to work as a team. Remember to pitch the pegs in line with the guyrope

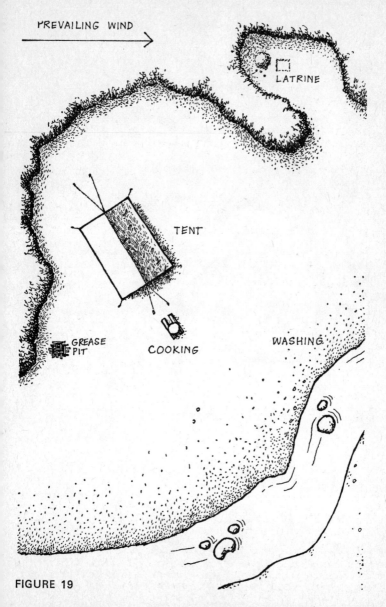

PREVAILING WIND

LATRINE

TENT

GREASE PIT

COOKING

WASHING

FIGURE 19

47

FIGURE 20

SPREAD TENT ON GROUND WITH DOOR
AWAY FROM WIND. PEG DOWN SIDES.

STONES OR SNOW

← WIND

ONE HOLDS DOOR END IN POSITION
THE OTHER PUTS IN PEGS AND GUYS

ERECTING A MOUNTAIN TENT

seams and do not tighten the guys too much in wet weather. A light polythene or plastic sheet is handy, if the rain beats in. It can cover the gear, or in an emergency, cover you.

SETTLING DOWN

Before settling down for the night, you need to have everything under cover, and secured against weather, pests and thieves.

Check all guys and tent pegs. Tent pegs should be hammered in at an angle of about 45°. Make sure the flysheet is not rubbing against the inner wall. Slacken or adjust the guys as necessary.

Muddy boots, empty sacks and pack frames, tinned food, can all be stowed outside, under the flysheet wall.

Open food should stay inside, otherwise it will attract rodents, and valuable equipment, cameras or binoculars need to be kept somewhere secure. Put shoes, torches, etc., near to hand, and in the same place every time. Then you will know where to find them in the dark.

You can leave most of your cooking gear outside, *after* you have cleaned them, and probably the stove as well. In cold weather you will need to keep your gas stoves and spare containers inside the tent. In the U.K. the gas available is butane which will not vapourise at −1°C. In the winter you will need propane. If you usually camp at altitude you should have a paraffin stove or lamp; keep the fuel outside the tent, away from naked flames, and again *never* fill stove or lamp inside the tent. Beware of fire, always.

SLEEPING

If you are using an air bed, don't inflate it too hard. Have some ventilation in the tent, and stow your spare gear around the sides of the tent and not in the middle. This is where a tent with walls comes into its own. You have much more storage space. Roll up spare clothing to make a pillow, and place gym shoes and torch somewhere ready to hand.

Wear as few clothes as possible in the tent and especially for sleeping. You will feel the benefit when you put them on in the morning. Sleep with your head near the entrance. This has many advantages. You get more air. You can read until it is really dark. You can have a look round if you hear intruders, and most important, you can brew up in the morning without leaving the bag. If rain comes in, you feel it on your head before it has soaked your bag.

FLIES, MOSQUITOES, CREEPY-CRAWLIES

Be you never so stoic, few things are more irritating than a night spent with a mosquito. You will have to share the air with insect life, but you can cut them down to a minimum.

A tent with a fitted groundsheet, and a zip-up flyscreen on the door is a good start.

Camp away from long grass, and hedges. Flying insects don't like breezes, and are to be found close to thick bush. At night a naked light, especially a Tilley lamp, will attract millions of moths and mosquitoes.

You can buy pellets and sprays to clear midges out of the tent and make it unpleasant for them. Various repellent creams are also available. In some parts of Scotland, for example, there is nothing for it but to get inside your tent after sundown.

Hygiene round the camp is also important. Flies will congregate round uncovered latrines, and scraps of food. Bury all the spoil, and as a final contribution to good living, keep yourself clean.

Chapter 12

CAMP COOKING

Many books on camping provide pages of recipes and jolly hints on how to make cakes and bake hedgehogs. This is just marvellous, and worth a book on its own. Since here we are concerned with basics you need—basically—to understand the rudiments of cooking.

The best teacher is mother, wife or girl friend, who can aquaint you with the time necessary to boil an egg (about four minutes once the water boils) and advise you on the type of food you are likely to be capable of cooking. Stews, good thick soups, and a good breakfast fry-up, will be the basic diet, but remember to include some fruit and a few milky puddings. You can do a lot with milk, honey and packet cereals, which are light and easily packed.

Cooking is by no means a feminine skill, all the best cooks being men, and there is no reason why, after a bit of practice, and given some commonsense, you cannot learn to cook a variety of dishes. Don't work to the rule 'when it's brown it's done, and when it's black it's burnt'!

COOKING SITE
The first job is to select a site for the cooking. In decent weather this needs to be on flat ground, sheltered from the wind and preferably with some higher flat surfaces around to rest the food on, or sit on while you are cooking; tree stumps, rocks or low stone walls are ideal.

Be certain the stove is firm in the ground. Support it with stones, or dig it in a little if needs be. You don't want it tipping over and depositing your food on the ground. The wind, even a light breeze, will blow the flame about, and greatly reduce the amount of heat on the cooking vessel, so shield the burner from the wind. Many stoves come equipped with shields, or have one available as an extra. If the weight is supportable they can be very useful.

COOKING TIPS
Keep it simple. When in doubt, boil water. With boiling water you can wash up, shave, wash, make tea, boil eggs, make coffee, cocoa, and a lot more. So if you have a spare burner, put some water on to boil.

If you are cooking food by immersing the tin in boiling water, don't forget to puncture the tin! If you let the contents boil without the steam escaping, you will generate a startling explosion. Beware of jumping fat. It can give you a very nasty burn. Don't let the fat get too hot. If your frying pan bursts into flames don't pour water into it. Just turn the stove off and cover the pan with a lid or damp cloth. Always stir soups or stews regularly. Don't forget to take salt, sugar and tin openers. Buy packaged or tubed foods rather than tins, whenever possible. Take your litter, including empty tins to a proper refuse bin.

WATER

If you take water from a stream or even an outside tap, it is better to boil it. You will get through a lot of water, and it is heavy to cart about. You will need at least a litre a day each and probably more. A pint of water weighs 20 ozs ($\frac{1}{2}$ kilo) and a litre weighs 43 ozs (1.25 kilos). So if you can, find safe local water and use it. You will need plastic bottles or a canvas bucket to carry it in.

FOUL WEATHER COOKING

To cook in strong winds or rain you will need some cover, probably in the flysheet porch of the tent. So remember to buy a tent with such a porch. This practice should only be used when absolutely necessary, as there is a small risk of setting the tent alight, and a large risk of spattering both tent and flysheet with fat, which will do it no good at all.

For the same reason, cooking inside the tent is to be discouraged. If you must do so, restrict your efforts to stews and tea. Flying fat will stink the place out for days, and get everywhere. Don't cook inside a tent with solid fuel. It gives off unpleasant fumes. Always have the tent well ventilated when cooking.

FOOD HYGIENE AND CLEANING UP

Wash your hands before cooking, and make everyone else do the same before eating. It's more civilised. (Dinner jackets need only be worn in the Tropics!) After the meal, clean all the dishes at once. Don't leave the food to harden on the plates.

Hot water can be used to swill off fat, but a much better method is to scour the plates with sand or earth, to absorb the fat, and the utensils can then be washed clean, even in cold water. Plastic plates and mugs are light, don't get too hot, and are easy to scour.

Small scraps of food, crusts, etc., can be widely scattered, but not within the camp area, for the birds. Any large scraps, bones, etc. should be buried. Tins, plastic wrappers, and any rubbish that cannot be eaten by animals, or buried to rot, *must* be taken home or placed in a proper refuse receptacle as soon as possible. For this purpose take with you two or three stout plastic bags. Beat tins flat with a stone, crush up packets and cartons, and stow them away until you find a dustbin. If you have stew or soup tins to dispose off, drain the unused liquid into a hole and bury it. The small solid scraps can be scattered for the birds. The golden rule is to keep the camp site **CLEAN.** Otherwise, you will attract flies, rats, and public contempt.

Chapter 13

STRIKING CAMP

Comes the day when it's time to go home. You awaken from a deep sleep, and horrors, rain is beating steadily on the canvas. This is one of the golden rules of camping, it always rains when you are puttng up or striking the tent.

ROUTINES

The important thing is to have a Routine.

You can, of course, stay in bed. Take a look out of the door, and if you have time and the sky is clearing, stay put.

If you have to move, then first stick to the normal routine. Have breakfast, and do as much preparation as possible. Our routine, rain or shine, is as follows. We assumed when we established it, that it *would* be raining. The object is to pack up quickly, and get as much dry gear as possible into our rucksacks.

TERRY: Gets fully dressed, leaves tent. Collects cooking gear, prepares and cooks breakfast and cleans plates and cooking gear.

ROB: Rolls up sleeping bags, deflates lilos, packs up rucksacks, and tidies inside of tent. Sees to it that by the time breakfast is ready, all is stowed away except breakfast and cooking gear and the tent. Then gets dressed for outdoors.

BOTH: Collapse tent guys, leaving flysheet. Place rucksacks in porch. detach tent guys, tent from poles, then roll up tent under the shelter of the fly. Finally, with tent stowed, the flysheet is collapsed with both keeping it out of the mud, shaken and stowed in a plastic bag, in a rucksack pocket. Pull out, wipe and stow tent pegs. Place rucksacks somewhere off the ground, sheltered if possible.

BOTH: Go to far side of camp site and walk across the ground several times picking up any rubbish. (Not just our own.) Fill in any holes, replacing turfs; trying to leave the site without any sign of our presence. We also found lost items this way, so there is self-interest in it as well.

BOTH: Go and thank farmer, manager or landowner, pay dues, and plod away.

How you collapse the tent depends on what sort of tent you are using. They come nowadays in all shapes and sizes. We, luckily, have a tent that can be detached from the poles and folded up inside the fly. If yours will not do this, then even so, leave the tent till last. It may stop raining, and you can pack it away in the dry.

Dry or not, you can use the tent to keep everything else dry, until you are ready to stow it.

If the day is fine, you will have fewer problems. Again leave the tent up, for the fly anyway will be beaded with dew, and there may be condensation on or in the tent. Let as much of this evaporate before you strike the tent.

Your mid-day halt, if fine, is not too soon to pitch the tent again, just to let it dry. Air the sleeping bag too.

Chapter 14

CARE AND MAINTENANCE

As we mentioned at the start of this book, camping equipment, even at basic levels, is not especially cheap. Given that you have bought robust equipment to begin with, it will, however, last you many years if you look after it properly.

The care and maintenance of your gear, is not a once a year thing.

THE TENT

You need to make a daily check of the tent, to see that seams and guys are standing up to the action of wind and rain. If a seam starts to unravel, have it sewn up quickly. Replace frayed guys, and hammer bent pegs straight again at the first opportunity.

PROOFING

Your tent can be holed by branches or sharp objects, and lose its proofing, either through long exposure to the weather or as the result of fat spattering on the fabric. If your tent is damaged in this way, consult a competent stockist. Patches of a suitable colour and material can be obtained, and there are proofing preparations and sprays on the market.

STORAGE

Before you stow your tent away, even for a short time, clean, dry and air it thoroughly.

We always put ours up in the kitchen after a trip, and leave them up overnight. This gets it dry and properly aired. Damp is the great enemy, leading to mildew and rot. During the winter try and hang the tent up, rather than roll it. If you have to roll it up, roll it loosely to let the air into the folds. Out of season, open it fully at least once a month and beware of moths and mice.

TENT PEGS

Straighten any bent ones, clean off any rust, and wipe with a lightly oiled rag. Stow rolled in newspaper.

GROUNDSHEETS

Repair any holes with adhesive tape. Get all the mud and dried grass off. Dust with French chalk.

SLEEPING BAGS

Unzip, turn inside out to air. If it is getting dirty, have it dry-cleaned. Dry-cleaning reduces the life of a bag, but not so much as ingrained dirt will. Wash, dry, and iron the inners.

STOVES AND COOKING AND EATING EQUIPMENT

Check the stoves over for worn parts. Clean jets, and replace washers around the burner and filling screw. Any gas containers should be checked for rust or damage.

Scour all the cooking and eating gear, and dry thoroughly. Wrap in newspaper.

LAMPS AND TORCHES
Check glass and replace if necessary. Remove batteries from torches. Even leak-proof ones seem to leak.

BOOTS, CLOTHING
Clean, and polish or oil boots. Shake out clothes, have repairs done, and be sure everything is clean and dry before you put it away. Beware of moth.

Finally, give everything a final check and stow away in one place where you will know where to find all of it, when next you need it.

Do all this as soon as you get home. Do not leave checks and maintenance for the next trip, let alone next year. Carry out your maintenance **after** the trip, not **immediately** before.

Chapter 15

FIRST AID AND SAFETY

MAP AND COMPASS

Anyone enjoying out of doors pursuits, especially in remote areas, will enjoy them even more, if he or she can look after him or herself. For the camper, the useful ancillary skill is a sound knowedge of map and compass work, survival and safety rules, and first aid.

You need up-to-date maps, a Silva Compass, and a sharp pencil. You also need to know how to use them. If you don't, get someone to teach you, or buy a copy of The Spur Book and Compass (75p), which gives all the basic information, and is available from all good bookshops.

In mountains or remote areas, you should also understand basic survival techniques (see Spur Book of Survival 1976). Carry a First Aid kit including a space blanket, have at least one companion, and tell someone where you are going. Carry survival

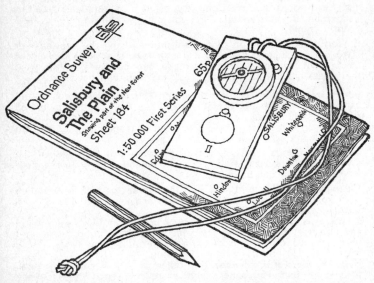

FIGURE 21

rations. These are simple precautions, but they are neither unnecessary nor childish. Only a fool fails to learn elementary skills and take simple precautions. Don't confuse 'toughness' with stupidity.

FIRST AID

You should purchase a First Aid kit, containing the following items: Bandages in two different widths, lint, Elastoplast, anti-sceptic cream, plasters, scissors, aspirin, calamine lotion, lip salve and a skin cream. Know how to give First Aid. Here are a few hints.

Blisters: These are best avoided by having soft, well-washed socks, and comfortable boots. If you get a blister, cover it with a plaster, but do not burst it.

Wind Burn: Faces that work indoors can be flayed by the wind when out of doors. Lips will crack and blister, Put on lip-salve and skin cream lightly for the first few days. It's not effeminate and avoids discomfort.

Cuts: The way to stop bleeding is pressure. Put on a pad of lint, and bind firmly over the cut. If blood soaks through, put on more lint. If the bleeding is very bad, apply pressure around the cut, and head for a doctor. Don't try using a tourniquet. They are dangerous. Beware of tetanus if you cut yourself on dirty ground or on rusty wire.

Broken Bones: These present a real problem, and the best answer is to get the injured party to a doctor fast. If a leg is broken, or the patient cannot be moved, make him comfortable, splinting the break, but not attempting to set the limb, and get help.

Burns: Immerse the burn in cold water. This will cool the flesh and help prevent blistering. If clothing catches fire, smother it, or roll to put out the flames.

Cover up the burns with a dry, clean bandage and get help. Do not smear the burn with fat or butter.

Bites and Stings: An anti-histamine cream will help reduce the swelling. If the sting is still deep in the wound, let a doctor remove it. A little iodine can be helpful.

Cleanliness: Few injuries are any the worse for a light sponging with soap and water. Get the dirt off, and keep the wound from turning septic.

Shock: A sudden injury, a bad cut or break, can leave the injured party in a state of shock. Treat for shock by making the patient lie down and keep warm, giving a warm drink (only if it is not an internal injury) and tryng to cheer him up.

Hypothermia (or Exposure): Hypothermia is loss of body heat, leading to unconsciousness and eventually death. It is usually brought on by tiredness, wet clothes and cold winds, or a combination of all three. In the mountains you should be aware of the ever present menace of hypothermia, and watch out for signs.

These are listlessness, falling behind on the march, slurred speech, double vision, and collapse.

The treatment is to get the victim out of the wind, and warm him up. Wrapping him in a space blanket is a good start, then brew a hot drink and get it into him.

The best cure is prevention, and if you wear warm windproof garments, eat regularly, and avoid getting over-tired, you should be all right.

Accidents do happen, and out of doors, doctors are usually more than a 'phone call away. You must therefore know about First Aid, and not be afraid to use it.

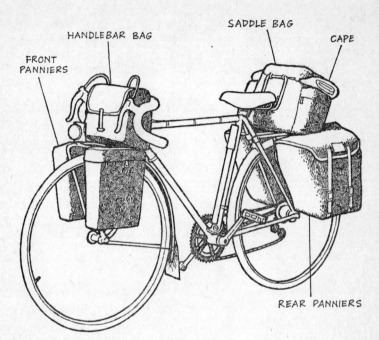

FRONT PANNIERS

HANDLEBAR BAG

SADDLE BAG

CAPE

REAR PANNIERS

SOME OF THE WAYS OF
CARRYING GEAR ON A CYCLE.

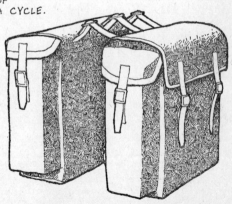

FIGURE 22

Y.H.A. 'SPECIAL' PANNIERS

Chapter 16

CAMPING BY BIKE AND BY BOAT

The amount of gear that can be carried is considerably increased if you travel by bicycle, canoe or boat. It is possible to cover quite a lot of ground in this way.

CYCLING

When camping by bicycle make sure that the brakes are in good condition and that the tyres are pumped up hard. The principle of load carrying differs somewhat to that for the rucksack, the object in this case being to keep the load low. A heavy rucksack worn on a bike will be far too top heavy. Some of the many excellent panniers and bags for cyclists are shown in Fig. 22.

CANOEING

Canoe expeditions are a subject in themselves and we only have space to mention some considerations.

Remember that if you are going to load a canoe with a lot of camping gear then you must have adequate buoyancy. You will of course wear a buoyancy aid or life-jacket as suitable (Fig. 23).

A two-seater touring canoe is the ideal craft for camping. Stow all gear which is to be kept dry in waterproof bags, it is sure to get wet if you don't. Articles should be stowed so that what you need first goes in last, i.e. tent. Check the trim of the canoe when loaded and adjust the load if necessary.

When making camp take the canoe out of the water and put up the tent in the usual way. You can dispense with the tent and use the canoe to bivouac if you are feeling rugged.

There are many areas where it is possible to camp by inland waters when using either a canoe or a boat. The Thames is very well provided with camp sites on its upper reaches and there are sites on the Norfolk Broads, The Lake District and many in Scotland and Wales.

BOATING

To camp on inland waters you can use punts, inflatables and rowing or sailing dingies by either mooring at the waters edge or by pulling the boat onto the bank and camping as described for canoeists.

If you wish to sleep on board, a twelve foot dinghy is about the smallest boat that will accommodate two people. The major limiting factor is if you can lie under the thwart comfortably. Remember that if you use an airbed, although this will keep you out of any bilge water, it will also raise you a couple of inches so a pad might be better.

The best cover is a properly made one as shown in Fig. 24, but the sail can be pressed into service for this role in a sailing dinghy. A gunter rigged craft will be found a more useful rig for camping

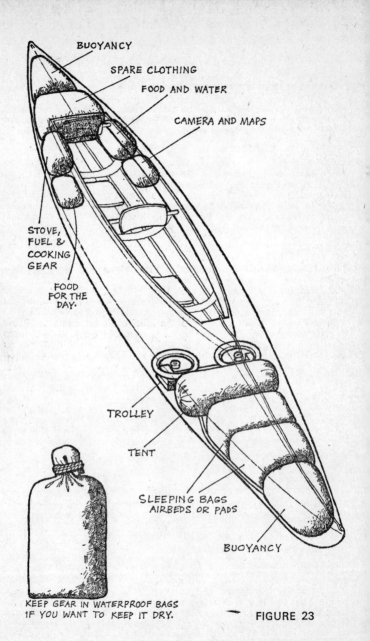

BUOYANCY

SPARE CLOTHING

FOOD AND WATER

CAMERA AND MAPS

STOVE, FUEL & COOKING GEAR

FOOD FOR THE DAY.

TROLLEY

TENT

SLEEPING BAGS AIRBEDS OR PADS

BUOYANCY

KEEP GEAR IN WATERPROOF BAGS IF YOU WANT TO KEEP IT DRY.

FIGURE 23

62

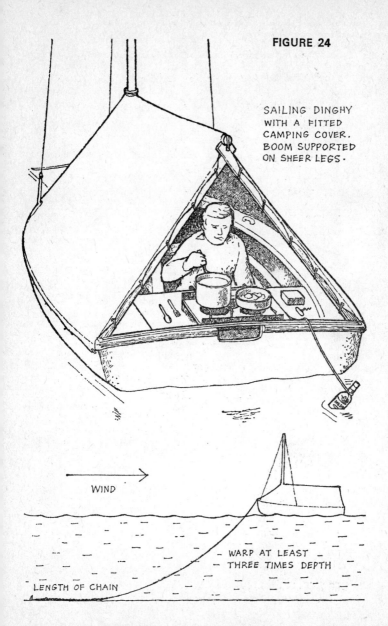

FIGURE 24

SAILING DINGHY
WITH A FITTED
CAMPING COVER.
BOOM SUPPORTED
ON SHEER LEGS.

WIND

WARP AT LEAST
THREE TIMES DEPTH

LENGTH OF CHAIN

than a bermudan one.

When lying at anchor you won't have gimbels to support your stove in a dinghy so you might find cooking impossible in anything other than a flat calm.

CONCLUSION

A knowledge of camping skills is essential to the outdoor man. Day trips lead to staying out overnight, and living in the open. No outdoor man can avoid it.

This book has, we hope, given the outdoor novice, whatever his sphere of outdoor activity, enough knowledge to start camping, and develop the basic information we have provided into the knowledge necessary for comfortable outdoor living, in accordance with his own particular taste. It's all up to you from then on, but that way, and the experience will come naturally.

Only practice and experience can teach you all you need to learn, and give you the know-how necessary to live outdoors, in remote or extreme conditions. Don't, we beg you, start your camping life on top of Cairngorm in mid-winter. Start in your own back garden. Leave Cairngorm until you are fully experienced. Don't be afraid to ask advice and take it.

You can equip yourself with all manner of equipment, but the best equipment is commonsense, experience, and a sense of humour. With all those and the right kit, you can go a long way, and good luck to you!